Little red hen and the water snake and What is it?

Hannie Truijens

**Little red hen and
the water snake**   page 2

What is it?   page 10

Nelson

Little red hen and the water snake

A little red hen made a nest by the river.
She laid a brown egg in her nest.
Then she went to look for food.

A water snake had his home
in the river.
He found the nest and ate
the brown egg.
"Yum yum that was good,"
he said.

The little red hen came back to her nest and found the egg gone.
The next day she laid another brown egg.
She flew into the tree to watch.

The water snake came and ate the egg.
"Yum yum that was good," he said.
"I have found the robber," said the little red hen.

"Let me trick that robber,"
she said.
The next day she looked for a
brown stone.
She put it in her nest.
Then she flew into the tree
to watch.

The water snake came for the egg.
He opened his mouth and in went
the brown stone.
It was cold and hard and it was
not good to eat.

The water snake went back to the river.
The stone made him very sick.
"Oh no," he said.
"That was a bad egg."

The next day the little red hen
laid another brown egg.
But the water snake didn't come
to eat it.
"I tricked that robber, didn't I?"
she said.

What is it?

Coco the parrot came to see the friends.
"Hello, hello," he said.
"How are you?"

Coco had a present for Deb.
"Thank you," said Deb.
"But what is it?"

Coco had presents for Meg and Ben.
"Thank you," they said.
"But what is it?"

Coco had presents for Jip
and Sam.
"Thank you," they said.
"But what is it?"

"This is to eat," said Coco.
"This is to put on.
This is to sleep on.

This is to play on.
And this is to put on
your head."

The friends had a present for Coco.
"Thank you," said Coco.
"But what is it?"